OTHER BOOKS BY GARY NEAL HANSEN

Kneeling with Giants:
Learning to Pray with History's Best Teachers

The Kneeling with Giants Reader:
Writings on Prayer by History's Best Teachers

The Small Group Leader's Guide
for Kneeling with Giants

And in the "Being Reformed"
adult curriculum series:

The Heidelberg Catechism
(Participant's Book)

Church History: Those Who Shaped the Faith
(Participant's Book)

LOVE YOUR BIBLE

Finding Your Way to the Presence of God
with a 12th Century Monk

Gary Neal Hansen

Scripture quotations are from the New Revised Standard Version Bible, copyright © 1989 National Council of the Churches of Christ in the United States of America. Used by permission. All rights reserved.

Cover design: Teddi Black

Cover image: Modified from "Roof Ladder," by Miguel Virkkunen Carvalho on Flickr (http://bit.ly/1xE7CoS), Licensed under Creative Commons, Attribution 2.0 Generic (https://creativecommons.org/licenses/by/2.0/)

Copyright © 2015 Gary Neal Hansen

All rights reserved.

ISBN-13: 978-0-9864124-0-0 (paper);
978-0-9864124-1-7 (ebook)

For Steve Hayner
With thanks for teaching me to love my Bible

Acknowledgments
1

Introduction
3

Chapter One: Reading
11

Chapter Two: Meditating
19

Chapter Three: Praying
27

Chapter Four: Contemplating
33

Conclusion
41

Before You Go...
49

Endnotes
51

ACKNOWLEDGMENTS

SPECIAL THANKS to Dawna Duff, always my first and best reader, for her helpful insights and encouragement. I am very grateful to my colleagues Tim Slemmons and Bradley Longfield, for reading and commenting on drafts of the manuscript, and Susan Forshey, for thought-provoking conversation on the topic of *lectio divina*. I want to express my sincere gratitude to two freelance professionals whose work made this a better book: Erin Bartels, who edited the text, and Teddi Black, who designed the cover. Thanks as well to Colin Hay, whom I've never met but whose vocals on my headphones, both solo and with Men at Work, somehow made the editing possible.

INTRODUCTION

YOU WANT to be competent and confident in your faith; you want a discipleship that goes deep into your life so it can go wide to the world. To get there, the first step is a solid working knowledge of the Bible. That is how you will be able to live, understand, and share what you believe. You need to love your Bible—or it will never be a life-giving resource.

The problem is this: a lot of us don't, in practical terms, love the Bible. We don't even read it. We don't know where to start. We love Jesus; we honestly love the biblical faith and try to live it.

We need a way to encounter the Bible that does more for our hearts than academic study, and that does more for our minds than devotional reading. We really need an approach to the Bible that helps us draw close to God to receive the new life he promises in Christ.

This little book is going to teach you that approach.

Many things hold us back: Some think only scholars can understand these ancient books from unfamiliar cultures. Some fear that if they open the Bible they will find a rulebook, a long list of "dos" and "don'ts." Some suspect the Bible is all about things that science has proven wrong.

Each of these is a false obstacle, at most a half-truth:

Yes, scholars can uncover some things that ordinary Christians won't find—but these are not the essential things. An ordinary Christian reading the Bible, without Greek or Hebrew, can learn a vast amount about God and life in harmony with him. That is what is central.

Yes, the Bible does affirm some things and disapprove of others—but the biblical faith is never about legalism. In Scripture, God always aims to help us toward an abundant life of freedom in loving relationship with him.

Yes, the biblical worldview reflects the science of past ages—but science does not touch the actual subject matter. Scripture is about God and human nature, and those haven't changed a bit.

All of these potential obstacles are about our

intellectual understanding of the Bible's contents. That means they stop short of what we should be aiming for.

When we open the Bible we should be aiming to know God better. God is the one whose actions the Bible records. God is the one who inspired the Scriptures, as Paul put it (2 Timothy 3:16), whose very breath sweeps through them so that they are useful for our growth. The God of the Bible is the one who can equip us with the faith and wisdom that we need in order to live as Christians.

So we need an intellectually rigorous and deeply prayerful approach to the Bible, to lead us step by step toward a direct and life-giving encounter with God. The good news is that such an approach has been around for over 1500 years, shaping the lives of some of the most effective disciples who ever lived.

In Latin it is called *lectio divina*. That means "divine reading," though it is sometimes rendered "spiritual" or "prayerful" reading. This kind of engagement with the Bible was a daily practice in medieval monasteries and convents. St. Benedict (c. 480—c. 545), the "father of Western monasticism," expected each monk to have a two-hour shift of *lectio divina* every day—and *two* daily shifts of it in the dark winter months.[1]

The great teacher of the practice came much later. He was an obscure Carthusian monk named Guigo II (d. 1188) who wrote a little book called *The Ladder of Monks*. He was so humble he didn't even put his name on it. But it has, ever since, been the go-to text for people who want to understand authentic *lectio divina*.

In Guigo's understanding, *lectio divina* was a four-step process: reading, meditating on, praying, and contemplating through a passage of Scripture. He portrays them as four rungs up a ladder—though he also describes *lectio divina* in metaphors of eating and construction. Here is his first summary of those steps:

> Reading is the careful study of the Scriptures, concentrating all one's powers on it. Meditation is the busy application of the mind to seek with the help of one's own reason for knowledge of hidden truth. Prayer is the heart's devoted turning to God to drive away evil and obtain what is good. Contemplation is when the mind is in some sort lifted up to God and held above itself, so that it tastes the joys of everlasting sweetness.[2]

Just naming the steps shows us that the whole person is involved. Two hours of reading, meditating, praying, and contemplating with

Scripture, every day, for years, would be transformative. Small wonder that so many monks became great missionaries and leaders for the Church in the Middle Ages.

And Guigo's sense of the potential benefits of the practice are serious too: he promises knowledge of hidden things, discernment of what is truly good, and a taste of God's everlasting sweetness. His four steps are all about the journey to the presence of God:

> These [steps] make a ladder for monks by which they are lifted up from earth to heaven. It has few rungs, yet its length is immense and wonderful, for its lower end rests upon the earth, but its top pierces the clouds and touches heavenly secrets.[3]

His original readers were monks, but what he teaches is useful for you and me too—for any Christian who wants the Bible to lead them closer to God.

Before we take a closer look at each of Guigo's steps, note how countercultural this approach to Scripture is. He does not settle for either the academic or the devotional options.

Guigo does not see engaging with Scripture as a *purely* intellectual task. Today Christians often try to approach the Bible like any other book, using just their own minds and the tools of literary and historical analysis. That could describe a professional scholar using the technical tools of higher criticism, or an ordinary Christian trying to understand the words, grammar, and context of a passage.

Don't get me wrong: those analytical tools are useful. However they are not the *whole* process. Guigo wants us to use our intellect to the fullest, but *lectio divina* has a bigger tool box. It brings more parts of the human person into an encounter with the Bible.

Guigo's process is also very different from *purely* devotional approaches to Scripture. It is even different from what passes for *lectio divina* in many circles today. He is not telling us to read the passage, listen for an evocative word or phrase, and quickly jump to an application. *Lectio divina* calls for more than our emotional reactions to the Bible.

Classical *lectio divina* is both important and helpful because it takes the Bible on its own terms: as an interface between God and humanity. That is what the Bible was for the great spiritual writers of the early centuries. Their commentaries and sermons show clearly that study of Scripture led to their own direct encounter with God.[4]

We need a lot from the Bible: we need it to help us become fluent in the basic elements of the faith, and we need it to lead us closer to God. That is what Guigo has in mind for us with *lectio divina*. The goal is not the Bible for its own sake. He wants us to wrestle with the Bible for the sake of knowing God.

Come along with me as we look at Guigo's ladder rung by rung. Let's take the first step.

CHAPTER ONE: READING

EVERY STEP of *lectio divina* uses different skills, drawing on a different part of you. The first rung of the ladder, according to Guigo, is reading. It sounds simple, but it isn't simplistic. This is not a Nike-influenced "*Just* read it!" Opening the book at Genesis and pressing on through to Revelation is an excellent practice for any Christian. It can be challenging, and it is a key way to get a working knowledge of Christianity, but it is not what Guigo is talking about.

So what is "reading" in *lectio divina*?

The first thing to note is that Guigo thinks small: the whole process of *lectio divina* can be practiced on a single verse of Scripture. Guigo uses one text—"Blessed are the pure in heart, for they shall see God" (Matt. 5:8)—as his example for every rung on the ladder.

This is because, to use my own metaphor, Guigo is a miner, not a map-maker. A map-maker would seek a bird's eye view of the length and breadth of the biblical landscape, undistracted by tiny details. At the very least he or she would chart a coherent unit—a whole Psalm or parable, a complete scene or argument from some biblical book.

Instead Guigo stays in one small area and drills down deep. As a miner he looks for what is underneath the surface, hoping to unearth valuable minerals or precious jewels. He will have to learn about the topside terrain too, but it is all for the sake of digging down.

Back to Guigo's ladder. When he steps onto the first rung, he aims to "read" his tiny text. As he said in the summary I quoted earlier, "Reading is the careful study of the Scriptures, concentrating all one's powers on it."

It is good that the process will start with careful study. Study is serious. It takes concentration and focus. We need to bring our whole minds to the process, even when the text is only a verse long.

Guigo sets clear goals for study in *lectio divina* —and very different goals than in purely academic study of Scripture. He is not aiming to discover what Mark or Luke sought to get across to one particular first-century Christian community. And he is not trying to puzzle out who drafted which fragment of Genesis or Isaiah before someone else compiled it into the book we know.

Instead, Guigo studies to find new life in Christ. He "seeks for the sweetness of a blessed life." Even reading, his first step with the Bible, is consciously about life in communion with God. He wants us to hunt for something to nourish our souls, because "Reading, as it were, puts food whole into the mouth."[5] We search for things that nourish a thriving life in Christ; that keeps study from becoming a heartless intellectual exercise.

Study of any kind is an effort to learn something, to answer questions. Guigo looks at his text—"Blessed are the pure in heart, for they shall see God"—and asks what its words mean. He asks how those words are used in the Bible. He asks how they connect with his life. From the answers he finds it is clear his questions were things like

- What is the "heart"?
- What does "purity" look like—and how does that compare to his own heart right now?
- What does it mean to "see" God?

He takes his time and digs down deep. Articulating the questions takes time. You have to stop and *not* read the rest of the passage, or the next chapter—at least not right away.

Probing for answers can be a short process or a long one. It might be a good time to get hold of some tools. If you go to BibleGateway.com (or if you have an old-fashioned concordance) you can look up all the places your verse's key words are used in the Bible. Looking up some of those texts you begin to absorb the range and depth of meanings the Bible attaches to the words.

Once you have poked around with your own study of a word, you can gain still more by looking it up in a good Bible dictionary. You'll find someone with a solid background presenting a synthesis of that word's meaning in Scripture, and that adds to your inner conversation.

If you are up for a challenge you can go even further with the reading process by trying find out how influential Christian thinkers of the past used the words. Pick a writer you are curious about: someone big, like Augustine (d. 430), the most influential theologian in the West; or John Calvin (d. 1564), who helped shape the Protestant Reformation. Then go to the Christian Classics Ethereal Library (www.CCEL.org) and find some of their works. Plug your word into the search window. Click on a few results and see what you find. (If you are at all like me you really need to keep it to two or three, or the whole afternoon will disappear into exploration.)

Then take stock. Open your journal, pick up a pen, and write some observations about what you've discovered. Write out your new working definitions of the key words in the verse. Spend a few sentences saying what these words mean in your experience. Tell the thoughts or stories that these words bring to mind. Think about what these words mean in our culture, and write that down too. Just a few minutes with a pen and paper will solidify the whole study process.

I hope you will give this kind of reading a try today. I suggest you start with the Psalms. These prayers and songs of God's ancient people are there to feed our souls by teaching us to pray, praise, and lament.

For an experiment, start at the very beginning of the Psalter, with the first verse of Psalm 1: "Happy are those who do not follow the advice of the wicked, or take the path that sinners tread, or sit in the seat of scoffers."

Read it. Reread it. Think of questions:

- ◆ What else does Scripture say about being "happy" or "blessed?" How does that compare with what our culture says?
- ◆ What else does Scripture say about "the

wicked," "sinners," and "scoffers?"

♦ What might the Psalmist mean by the different nuances in "following the advice," "taking the path," and "sitting in the seat" of these problematic people?

Dig into the terms. Ponder how the Bible uses them. For this verse, be sure to explore the Sermon on the Mount. And don't overlook the book of Proverbs. Consider your own life and culture. Augustine has a lot to say about the "blessed" life if you are curious, and a little brave. Give some time to study.

Near the end of the book Guigo re-emphasizes that reading is just the start of a bigger process. And it is good that there are three more rungs: study feels dry and dusty to a lot of people. They will be glad that there are still more and different approaches to come. Study can create other problems for those who do like it: if people end up convinced that they have all the answers, then study may have made them arrogant. Since there still is a long way to go, Guigo's approach keeps the overconfident humble.

He switches to a building metaphor to express this. "Reading comes first, and is, as it were, the foundation; it provides the subject matter we must use for meditation."[6] Laying a foundation is crucial, but it is not the end. You need the foundation to be strong—but it is useless if you don't go ahead and put up a building. You need to build walls and floors above the foundation.

The next step—meditation—is going to start that construction process.

CHAPTER TWO: MEDITATING

GUIGO SAYS the second step of *lectio divina* is meditation. He is going to describe a very particular, and very Christian, practice. Before diving into how it works, let me clarify what he does and doesn't mean.

The word "meditation" has a number of meanings, and the connotations can be troublesome. To some, meditation means trying to empty your mind of every thought; that can seem either impossible or contrary to God's intention in giving us the Word. To others, meditation means endlessly repeating a "mantra"—a secret word in a foreign language given by one's meditation teacher—which smacks of either idolatry or New Age silliness.

What about a third option? Raise your hand if "meditation" makes you think of a cow. Okay, if you are reading this in a public place you don't need to raise your hand.

Seriously, though. Meditation *should* make you think of a cow. It would have, if you were a Christian in the Middle Ages. For medieval monks and nuns, meditation was not about an empty mind. Meditation was something you did with a passage of Scripture. The meaning was very close to "rumination." As in "ruminant." You know: a cow. Think, "chewing her cud."

Study is a start for *lectio divina*—but it is just a start. You need to get enough Scripture into your mouth so that you can do something useful with it. Then you have to bite down, or you are missing something crucial. In the next step, "meditation chews it and breaks it up."[7]

Here is the classic process of Christian meditation from the Middle Ages: Take a verse of Scripture. Repeat it to yourself. Repeat it again. And again. And again and again and again. Chew your cud. Swallow the juice. Repeat it some more. There is nothing non-Christian about this kind of meditation. You are just repeating Scripture, chewing on God's Word.

Taking time to ruminate is important. If you travel to France and splurge on a restaurant with a couple Michelin stars, you are going to chew every single bite. If you don't, you'll waste a lot of money. You will miss a world of rich and complex flavors. And instead of nourishment you will probably get indigestion.

The same is true for Scripture. You need to chew if you want to enjoy or benefit from what study has put in your mouth. Just reading and moving on, even to read some more, can mean you miss out on something crucial. You need to chew with care so you get everything God put in the text for the good of your soul. And you don't want to try to swallow chunks that are too big and tough to get down.

With reading, or study, Guigo was just getting rolling. After chewing on his text he was so excited that his metaphors collided:

> Do you see how much juice has come from one little grape, how great a fire has been kindled from a spark, how this small piece of metal, 'Blessed are the pure in heart, for they shall see God', has acquired a new dimension by being hammered out on the anvil of meditation?[8]

If we take his metaphors seriously, meditation may be harder work than reading; it takes a blacksmith's strength to hammer on an anvil, and that is what he says meditation is about. Meditation is work, because all that repetition is an effort to learn something from the passage.

Guigo distinguishes meditation from study,

but sometimes it sounds like just another *kind* of study. As he said early on (with a little emphasis added), "Meditation is the *busy application of the mind* to seek with the help of *one's own reason* for knowledge of hidden truths."[9] That sounds like hard mental work. Clearly meditation is more than staring blankly into space. Two bits of good news: even if it is work it is doable; and it is well worth the effort.

My picture of Guigo as a miner helps again. A miner goes down through layers of the earth, finding different kinds of minerals in each one. This kind of meditation digs in the Bible to turn up "hidden truths." The first shovelful will turn up the passage's literal, historical meaning. Dig a bit deeper and up comes some guidance for our moral life. In goes the spade again, and we turn up insight into our spiritual journey toward God. Still further down we may unearth things that point to the hope of the coming Kingdom.

All those kinds of meanings were expected by medieval monks and scholars. They sought and found many layers in Scripture. They were convinced God wanted to convey a range of useful meanings in any given text—some meanings were merely historical, but others were moral, doctrinal, or about our life with God now and beyond history.

Again, this is countercultural. In our post-

Reformation and post-Enlightenment world, we have been raised to believe that any passage of Scripture has one, and only one, meaning. We look only for the idea the human author intended to get across to the original readers.

Searching for the author's intended meaning is important and useful—especially for those teaching and preaching on Scripture. But Guigo and the rest of the medieval Church were on to something important as well: God has more to say than the simple literal meaning of any given text conveys. Because God is actively present in our encounter with Scripture, he can speak personally to us about things well beyond what a preacher would focus on in preaching to a congregation. Meditation, or rumination, is the stage of *lectio divina* that brings out those layers of meaning.

Once you start to chew on a passage of Scripture, letting it run through your mind over and over, you come to know it intimately, viscerally. When you get to know a piece of music deeply, you start to hear melodic patterns and harmonies that the individual notes didn't convey. Similarly, meditation brings out those inner patterns and textures in Scripture that speak to spiritual life, moral progress, and other things God cares about.

As you meditate, you find yourself hearing what God is saying about the life he intends and promises. You start to consider your own life in relation to this rich message of the text. You begin to sense the distance between your reality and God's promise. That's good. Seeing the distance between here and the goal prompts a sense of longing that you will need in order to move forward.

So go back to Psalm 1:1, "Happy are those who do not follow the advice of the wicked, or take the path that sinners tread, or sit in the seat of scoffers." Take some time and chew on the same text you asked all those questions of a few minutes ago.

Repeat it over and over. Try repeating it without looking. When you have it by rote, keep repeating it. When you don't even have to think about it, keep repeating. Give it some time.

While the text repeats over and over, let your focus turn to the way it portrays God's call to faithful life. With the text constantly in the background, think about your current life, your relationships, your work, your aspirations.

- Whose voices have been giving you *advice*?
- What is the *path* you have been following?
- Whose *seat* are you sitting in—aspiring to be or keeping company with in your heart?

As your repeat the text, you may find yourself thinking about the simple meaning of the passage in its context. Your mind may drift to the moral or ethical choices you need to make, or how you tend to make them. Your mind may turn to your intimate connection to God. You may end up listening to the passage in relation to life struggles, death and loss, and your sense of hope in Christ.

Where do you find yourself, right now, in relation to this passage's vision of God's call? Notice the distance. Mark the obstacles.

Chewing lets you begin to see the richness of Scripture's meaning. Let your heart begin to long for the reality Scripture promises. Attend to the distance from here to heaven, and the aching emptiness that needs filling.

Meditation makes us aware of how far our own experience of God and salvation are from what Scripture promises. That should prompt us to ask God's help in getting there—reaching for the third rung on the ladder, which is prayer.

CHAPTER THREE: PRAYING

THE THIRD rung on Guigo's ladder is prayer. You do not put away the Bible and then start to pray. This kind of prayer is something you do with a passage of Scripture. Studious reading leads you into meditative chewing, and that whole process prompts you to start praying the text.

That is counterintuitive for a lot of Christians. Many who spend regular time with God will tell you that they encounter Scripture and pray, but as two completely distinct disciplines.

That often makes perfect sense. Across the centuries and around the world, Christians have developed many rich ways of praying. I explore ten of them in my book *Kneeling with Giants: Learning to Pray with History's Best Teachers*, and many of these ways of praying can be practiced without a Bible in hand.

Guigo, though, is focusing on one particular way of praying as part of *lectio divina*. It is another way to wrestle with a passage of Scripture.

An encounter with Scripture really should be a kind of prayer. If Scripture is God's Word, then it is the place where God tries to communicate with us. That makes reading the Bible a way of listening for God. Long before you speak a word in prayer, God has begun the conversation. He is waiting for you to hear and respond.[10]

Another way to consider the Bible's natural connection to prayer is to think of Scripture like glass. As if looking in a mirror, the Bible reflects our lives, with all our brokenness and failings. What we see prompts us to ask for mercy. Or as if looking through a window into heaven, in Scripture we catch glimpses of God's character and purposes. What we see nudges us to pray for God's will to be done in the world and our lives.

We've seen that, in Guigo's description, *lectio divina* is a way to take the passage slowly, and dive in deep. Reading brings clarity; meditation invites self-examination. We catch a vision of God's intention for us, some part of life made whole and holy by intimacy with God. Seeing just how far current life is from that goal leads to confession and longing. We are ready to pray for God's help in reaching what the text promises.

To put it another way, part of what reading and meditation show as God's intention is that God is present, eager to help. Any real clarity about your current progress is built on God's grace, which equips you to ask for his help to take the next step.

So you pray: you call out to God and ask him to bring about the fullness of what you now know to be his vision for you. In Guigo words, "Reading seeks for the sweetness of a blessed life, meditation perceives it, prayer asks for it."[11]

He takes his food metaphor a couple of different ways as he explores how reading, meditating, and praying relate to each other.

With that juicy grape, after you put it in your mouth, you chew and chew, and then "prayer extracts its flavor."[12] You pray the biblical text to suck out all its juicy goodness. You will not swallow food that doesn't impact your taste buds.

He also shifts his metaphor to some kind of thick skinned fruit. Prayer and meditation take us through two tough outer layers: "Reading works on the outside, meditation on the pith."

If Guigo had been in the tropics he might have been describing a coconut. With hard work you hack through the outer layers, but you are left hungry and thirsty. A seemingly impenetrable shell stands between you and the sweet stuff inside. If you don't have a machete, hammer, or drill, you need to ask for some help. So in the third step, "prayer asks for what we long for."[13]

Again Guigo gives examples from his own *lectio divina* on "Blessed are the pure in heart, for they shall see God."

His reading has shown him a new goal: the possibility of seeing God. His meditation has sobered him about how far he is from the call: his heart is not pure. He could never, on his own, become someone so blessed as to gaze on the beauty of the Lord. He has become awestruck by the goal, filled with longing.

And so he prays for God's help. As he prays he remembers another passage: he sees himself in the role of the woman who sought Jesus and was turned away as a foreigner. She shot back that the even the dogs got to eat the children's crumbs that fell from the master's table (Matthew 15:21-28).

Taking her as his model (and with a touch of the rich man in Luke 16:24), Guigo asks for sheer mercy. He calls out to God, "So give me, Lord, some pledge of what I hope to inherit, at least one drop of heavenly rain with which to refresh my thirst, for I am on fire with love.[14]" He asks to truly know God, knowing that will only happen if God purifies his heart.

Read and meditate until you know you need what Scripture offers. Then pray for help to obtain it. That is the meaning of praying Scripture for Guigo. You are ready to start when you feel the gap between your life and God's promise. Then praying is the obvious thing to do.

So go back to Psalm 1:1 and spend some time praying it. You have asked questions about it and studied for answers. You have ruminated on it and weighed your life in its balance. Now go to it again and ask God's help. Let the verse become the substance of your conversation with God.

"Happy are those who do not follow the advice of the wicked, or take the path that sinners tread, or sit in the seat of scoffers."

What do you need to reach the fullness of what God promises there?

- ◆ Do you need to ask for genuine God-given happiness, the blessed life?
- ◆ Do you need God's mercy because of having followed the wrong path?
- ◆ Do you need God's guidance about the company you keep or the aspirations of

your heart?

You discerned the gap between God's call and your life. Your prayer puts words on your soul's longing to bridge that gap.

Reading. Meditating. Praying. They are all connected. Each one is a separate way of engaging with a passage of Scripture, and each one pushes you on to the next.

And what would happen if God answered that prayer? That is where contemplation enters the picture.

CHAPTER FOUR: CONTEMPLATING

GUIGO CALLS the fourth and final step of *lectio divina* "contemplation." Here is his definition: "Contemplation is when the mind is in some sort lifted up to God and held above itself, so that it tastes the joys of everlasting sweetness."[15]

In its root meaning, contemplation means looking at something. Contemplative prayer is about gazing toward God. Guigo has chosen his example text well, since it says the pure in heart *see* God. Whatever the passage, though, the last step of *lectio divina* is contemplation on a text of Scripture.

When I was a child, my grandmother lived on the eleventh floor of an apartment tower on a hill overlooking downtown Tacoma. She loved the view of the ships coming and going, far below in Commencement Bay.

I wanted to go still higher. Every chance I got, I would take the elevator to the seventeenth floor. One more flight of stairs led to a heavy steel door. With a heave and a screech, it would open, and I would step out onto the roof. The bay and the city were below and the great dome of the sky above.

Awesome. It is an overused word these days, but still: it was awesome.

In this last step of *lectio divina*, you have your hands on the top rung of Guigo's ladder. You push your head up and look around. At least in terms of Guigo's metaphor, you are coming right into heaven. You pray for God to bring about the reality Scripture promises. God answers. You are in the presence of the living God, and now you see from a whole new perspective.

Even more awesome.

Guigo teaches that contemplation finally lays hold of the things reading and meditation made you aware of, and that you asked for in prayer. In his favorite food metaphor, where reading, meditating, and praying were putting food in your mouth, chewing it up, and enjoying the taste, "contemplation is the sweetness itself which gladdens and refreshes."[16]

Prayer *extracted* the flavor. Contemplation *is* the flavor. It is that inexpressible thing that happens when your taste buds come into contact with something wonderful.

So is contemplation a rooftop escape from the gritty problems of life down on ground level? Some think so, and they shy away from contemplative prayer. But actually contemplation is not escaping anything. Contemplation is finding something: the presence of God.

Better, though, to say that contemplation is when God *finds us*. It is not as if we have achieved something in these steps, climbing into God's presence by our own hard work. God comes to us as a sheer gift, the gracious answer to prayer.

We start to pray, as Guigo says,
> But the Lord . . . does not wait until the longing soul has said all its say, but breaks in upon the middle of its prayer, runs to meet it in all haste . . . and He restores the weary soul, He slakes its thirst, He feeds its hunger, He makes the soul forget all earthly things.[17]

God is eagerly waiting to bring us into the reality promised in Scripture: life intimately connected to him, in harmony with his purposes revealed in Christ. The whole subject matter is the blessed life, and "contemplation tastes it." When comparing *lectio divina* to digging through the tough outer layers of that mysterious fruit, "contemplation gives us delight in the sweetness which we have found."[18]

God turns our inward gaze to the life we were created for. It is a reorientation; it is also deeply disorienting. The soul forgets its needs and problems, as well as its ordinary joys. It is no accident if that sounds like the soul has had a few too many. God is giving the soul new life, "and by making it drunk He brings it back to its true senses."[19]

It may feel to some that Guigo has changed his tune: reading, meditating, and praying were all things that *we* could do with a biblical text. Now he tells us that contemplation is something *God* does. Does that mean that *lectio divina* is actually just a three-step process?

Yes and no.

In classical writings on the spiritual life, there are two kinds of contemplation. One form we simply receive from God. St. Teresa of Ávila (d. 1582) calls this "infused" contemplation, since God pours it into our lives from outside—usually when we are well along in the spiritual journey. Also, though, there are forms of contemplation that we take up intentionally and practice. Teresa describes these as "acquired" contemplation.[20]

Both the passive and the active forms of contemplation are relevant to *lectio divina*.

Guigo describes contemplation as God coming to answer the prayer of step three, and we receive it passively, as a gift. It comes from outside, but it is not independent of what we do. In one sense he is saying contemplation comes at the culmination a process: it is rarely given unless we go through the first three steps. In another sense he is describing each step as something suited to a particular stage of our growth. Reading, he says, is "proper to beginners," meditation is for "proficients," prayer for "devotees," and finally contemplation for "the blessed."[21]

Seeing contemplation as a gift is a wise reminder that every part of our salvation, including God's presence with us, comes by grace. It would be a bad sign if taking up contemplative prayer made us proud of ourselves and our spiritual maturity.

On the other hand, the fourth stage of *lectio divina* can also include contemplative practices. I want to describe two. One is from a teacher long after Guigo: St. Ignatius of Loyola (d. 1556), the founder of the Jesuit order. Ignatius taught a practice of turning our inward gaze onto the world of the biblical text. He called this "the prayer of the senses" and in it one goes slowly, meditatively, through a biblical story using each sense in turn.[22]

Ignatius has you start by exploring what your eyes see in a biblical scene. You take the details mentioned in the text as the starting point, but you go on to the many other things you might have seen if you had been there. Then you go back through the text, imagining what you could have heard in the scene, whether words spoken or other sounds—and so on through all five senses.

In your *lectio divina* on Psalm 1:1 you could practice contemplation by adapting this prayer of the senses. Entering the text with your mind's eye, you could try to see those paths that sinners go on, and the chairs that those scoffers are offering you. You could listen to hear what the voices of the wicked sound like, and the words they are trying to make you hear. You could try to feel in your body the joy of not going those troubled ways, or see the expressions on the faces of the blessed people the Psalmist describes.

Another way to approach the text contemplatively, whatever the words of the passage, is to stand, spiritually and imaginatively, within the text's world and turn your gaze toward God. Having studied, and ruminated, and called out to God about the message of this passage, you are deeply invested in it. In the ladder image of Guigo's book, you have climbed up high where you can see. It should make you aware of ways this passage of Scripture touches all parts of you—mind, heart, and body. So you stay there, inside that text, and you look toward God, the only one who can answer your prayer.

In this sense, contemplation really is the fourth step of the ladder. Having prayed your chosen passage of Scripture, you stay with it, turned toward God, and waiting, trusting God for the answer. And sometimes, either in the moment or afterward, looking back, you find that God has indeed brought you into that reality.

The building metaphor works as well as Guigo's ladder: Reading lays the building's foundation, as he said. Then come the floors where you do your daily living—meditation is like the ground floor, with the kitchen and dining room to feed you. Prayer is upstairs where your bedroom and home office are, private places to rest or focus on your calling. Contemplation is up on the roof. You don't have to sit on the roof to enjoy your house or find it useful. And you can't spend all your time up there; you go up knowing you will come back down. But, if you do climb onto the roof on a clear night, you can reach out and almost touch the stars.

You can live a whole lot of your Christian life without reaching out and touching the realities that Scripture talks about. You can even be happily engaged with Scripture through reading, meditation, and prayer, without that mysterious encounter. But if you want direct contact with what Scripture teaches—as much of the blessed life as a human being can bear—then you need to climb the lower rungs and take that fourth step.

Now that we are here on the top rung there is one more thing to consider. Think about that image of a ladder in Scripture: The patriarch Jacob, running for his life, stopped for a rest. While he slept he had a vision of "a ladder set up on the earth, the top of it reaching to heaven; and the angels of God were ascending and descending on it" (Genesis 28:12). Christian spiritual writers have made a great deal of that vision and image. Notice one thing: it is not a one way journey, even for the angels. The ladder is there for constant movement between earth and heaven.

How, then, will we make this ladder, *lectio divina*, an ongoing part of our own journey of faith—the never ending movement up to God and back down to the world?

CONCLUSION

GUIGO GOT to the heart of his message when he called his book *The Ladder of Monks*. He might have gotten still more across with *The Spiral Staircase of Monks*, since the journey goes ever upward and around again, but maybe that wasn't so catchy. Plus, he didn't ask me.

He is emphatic that each step is vital to the others. Three times he stands with his feet on two separate rungs, looking up and down to see why both are necessary[23].

On the first rung he notes that "reading without meditation is sterile." All that study he calls "reading" is just an intellectual exercise unless you chew it up and make it part of you. And then the flip side: "meditation without reading is liable to error." If you just chew on a passage out of context, without grasping its place in Scripture's message, you could end up believing all kinds of odd and erroneous things.

Second, one more step up, he tells us "prayer without meditation is lukewarm." If you try to seek what you need from God without knowing what God says life is about, your prayer is only half-baked. But then again, "meditation without prayer is unfruitful." If you do meditate on Scripture, but stop short of asking God to help you find the life Scripture promises, you've wasted your time.

Finally, coming to the top, "prayer when it is fervent wins contemplation, but to obtain it without prayer would be rare, even miraculous." Contemplation comes, essentially, as God's answer to our prayer for what Scripture promises; seek God earnestly, with heartfelt passionate prayer, and God comes in person. Of course Jesus could come and meet you without you seeking him, as he did for Paul. Miracles happen—but that is not the way it usually works.

To take the process in reverse,

- God wants to give you himself, Jesus, in contemplation.
- God grants his presence and new life only if you ask in prayer.
- You will only be moved to ask if you meditatively chew on what Scripture

teaches.

- You can only chew it after you put it in your mouth by faithfully, studiously, reading it.

Every step is necessary to move to the next level. Every step brings you closer to the goal: the presence of Jesus.

You do not take one quick trip through these four steps. Like a spiral staircase, you keep going up and around. Or maybe it is more like the instructions on the back of your shampoo bottle: "Lather, rinse, repeat." You read, and meditate, and pray—and you get a taste of Christ's presence. However, you do not get to remain forever in that holy intimacy. In contemplation Christ draws close, but then he seems to hide himself. Guigo suggests that this is intentional, since too much of Jesus' intoxicating presence could make us prideful or complacent about our progress.

Jesus wants to lead us through the process again, in a journey of real transformation. Guigo imagines Jesus saying,

> See now, you have had a little taste of how sweet and delightful I am, but if you wish to have your fill of this sweetness, hasten after me . . . lift up your heart to where I am at the right hand of God the Father. There you will

> see me not darkly in a mirror but face to face.[24]

He is still near, have no doubt. But we find we have to ascend the staircase again.

- ◆ Again we read.
- ◆ Again we meditate.
- ◆ Again we pray.
- ◆ Again we contemplate.

And time after time after time, we find ourselves in the presence of Jesus.

But remember what he said at the very beginning: he called the four rungs of this ladder "exercises." To add one last metaphor, think of the steps of *lectio divina* like the exercises that help you master a sport. Your coach makes you go through lessons and exercises in careful order, fully knowing that the order disappears come game time.

Take tennis. You practice the forehand groundstroke for your whole first lesson. Second lesson: backhand. Over time you pick up the volley, lob, and smash. You spend hours on your serve. You learn each shot in isolation, practicing in the order given by your coach. But in an actual game a serve is followed by a backhand, then a couple quick volleys, and another backhand. You practice each shot separately to be ready to move from one to another seamlessly as needed.

Same thing goes for *lectio divina*. It will be useful to take the four steps in order, giving time to each one. But once you understand each one, and the whole process, from experience, the order in which you need them may be as varied as the order of strokes in a tennis game.

This point goes a bit beyond Guigo, to be frank. He emphasizes that the higher steps depend on the lower, saying

> These degrees are so linked together, each one working also for the others, that the first degrees are of little or no use without the last, while the last can never, or hardly ever, be won without the first.[25]

His point is that one must do all four or we won't benefit—but he at least hints that one might sometimes reach the higher rungs outside the prescribed order.

My advice is to learn the process well and then live in freedom. Some will always take the steps in order. Some will eventually move between them as needed. Either way, over time, do them all and continually you will draw close to Jesus.

That is how Scripture can be life-giving to us. Getting doctrinal clarity from Scripture is really important—but if you stop when you reach doctrinal clarity, you are settling for something far too small. We come to really love the Bible when we know that it leads us, over and over, to Jesus and the new life he promises. It was true in the 12th century when Guigo wrote *The Ladder of Monks*. It is true today when it is so countercultural.

I asked you to try out each of Guigo's four steps of *lectio divina* on the first verse of the first Psalm. That was not a random choice. Though you can practice *lectio divina* on any passage of the Bible, the Psalms are a particularly rich place to start. They are the divinely approved prayers of God's people. Going through them slowly will invite you to bring more of yourself to God, and to see more clearly what life in him looks like.

If you decide to take one verse every day you will spend an excellent six and a half years in the Psalter. If that sounds like more than you bargained for, then you haven't quite heard Guigo's point or mine: this is about finding an ongoing, life-giving approach to Scripture that feeds you and strengthens you for the very long haul. This is not a short term program you try out and move on to the next thing. If you really come to understand *lectio divina* from the inside you won't want to be done with it—just as even after a really good meal you'll still come back later with an appetite.

You will surely explore Scripture in other

ways as well, even if you take up *lectio divina* as an ongoing practice. That is good. *Lectio divina* will make sure you keep coming back to the God who inspired Scripture in the first place.

Go ahead: dare to engage Scripture more passionately and prayerfully than academic approaches invite—because with *lectio divina* you read Scripture to enter God's presence. Dare to engage Scripture more intellectually and theologically than devotional approaches invite —because *lectio divina* requires you to study, and question, and think with all your being, on the way to encountering God.

Dare to go up the ladder, step by step, toward Jesus.

Step by step by step.

BEFORE YOU GO...

IF YOU enjoyed this journey into a great mentor from the Christian past, you'll love my book, *Kneeling with Giants: Learning to Pray with History's Best Teachers* (InterVarsity Press, 2012).

I explore ten classic ways Christians have practiced prayer down through the centuries and across all branches of the Church—Lutheran, Reformed, Catholic, Orthodox, Evangelical, and Charismatic—guided by great teachers who developed or exemplified each approach.

**Buy it on Amazon.com:
http://bit.ly/KneelingWithGiants**

ENDNOTES

[1] *RB 1980: The Rule of St. Benedict in English*, ed. Timothy Fry (Collegeville: The Liturgical Press, 1982) ch. 48, pp. 69-70.

[2] *Guigo II: Ladder of Monks and Twelve Meditations*, translated with an introduction by Edmund College and James Walsh (Kalamazoo: Cistercian Publications, 1979). 68.

[3] *Ladder of Monks*, 68.

[4] See Bernard McGinn's *The Foundations of Mysticism: Origins to the Fifth Century,* vol. 1 of The Presence of God: A History of Western Christian Mysticism (New York: Crossroad, 2004).

[5] *Ladder of Monks*, 68-69.

[6] *Ladder of Monks*, 79.
[7] *Ladder of Monks*, 69.
[8] *Ladder of Monks*, 71.
[9] *Ladder of Monks*, 68.
[10] This point is made beautifully in *Prayer* by Hans Urs von Balthasar (New York: Sheed & Ward, 1961), 12-13.
[11] *Ladder of Monks*, 68.
[12] *Ladder of Monks*, 69.
[13] *Ladder of Monks*, 69.
[14] *Ladder of Monks*, 73.
[15] *Ladder of Monks*, 68.
[16] *Ladder of Monks*, 69.
[17] *Ladder of Monks*, 73-74.
[18] *Ladder of Monks*, 68-69.
[19] *Ladder of Monks*, 74.
[20] Teresa makes the distinction in *The Way of Perfection* and you can find a discussion of it in my chapter on her in *Kneeling with Giants: Learning to Pray with History's Best Teachers* (Downers Grove: InterVarsity Press, 2012)
[21] *Ladder of Monks*, 80.
[22] He introduces this in his *Spiritual Exercises*, and I describe it in detail in my chapter on Ignatius in *Kneeling with Giants: Learning to Pray with History's Best Teachers*.
[23] *Ladder of Monks*, 82.
[24] *Ladder of Monks*, 78.

[25] *Ladder of Monks*, 80.

www.ingramcontent.com/pod-product-compliance
Lightning Source LLC
Chambersburg PA
CBHW052030290426
44112CB00014B/2453